The Orangutan

A Dillon Remarkable Animals Book

The Orangutan

By Ruth Ashby

DILLON PRESS
New York

Maxwell Macmillan International
Toronto

Maxwell Macmillan International
New York   Oxford   Singapore   Sydney

Acknowledgments

The author wishes to thank Dr. Gary Shapiro, vice president and treasurer of the Orangutan Foundation International, for his assistance.

Photo Credits

Photo research by Debbie Needleman
Cover courtesy of A. Peter Margosian, Photo/Nats
Back cover courtesy of David Stone, Photo/Nats

Jesse Cohen, National Zoological Park, Smithsonian Institution: frontispiece, 15, 23, 36; James Martin: title page, 20; Tim Laman, The Wildlife Collection: 8, 16, 32-33, 40; Suzanne Yin, Earthwatch: 13; A. Peter Margosian, Photo/Nats: 14; Jim Tuten, Busch Gardens Tampa: 24; Orangutan Foundation International: 26; Sydney Karp, Photo Nats: 28; James Gale: 39; Ione Rice, Earthwatch: 45, 55; Ann Tompkins, Earthwatch: 48; Cynthia Wilford, Earthwatch: 52

Book design by Carol Matsuyama

Library of Congress Cataloging-in-Publication Data

Ashby, Ruth.
 The orangutan / by Ruth Ashby. —1st ed.
   p. cm. — (Remarkable animals series)
   Includes bibliographical references (p.) and index.
   Summary: Describes the physical characteristics, habitat, and life cycle of the orangutan, including information on why the species is threatened and what is being done to save it.
   ISBN 0-87518-600-9
   1. Orangutan—Juvenile literature. 2. Endangered species—Juvenile literature. 3. Wildlife conservation—Juvenile literature. [1. Orangutan. 2. Rare animals. 3. Wildlife conservation.] I. Title. II. Series.
   QL737.P96A84   1994
   599.88' 42—dc20   93-5754

Dillon Press   Maxwell Macmillan Canada, Inc.
Macmillan Publishing Company   1200 Eglinton Avenue East
866 Third Avenue   Suite 200
New York, NY 10022   Don Mills, Ontario M3C 3N1

Macmillan Publishing Company is part of the Maxwell Communication Group of Companies.

First edition

Printed in the United States of America
10 9 8 7 6 5 4 3 2 1

Contents

Facts about the Orangutan

Scientific Name: *Pongo pygmaeus*
Description:
Height—Male: 4 to 5 feet (1.2 to 1.5 meters); female: 3½ feet (1.06 meters)
Weight—Male: up to 220 pounds (99.8 kilograms); average 165 pounds (74.9 kilograms); female: almost 90 pounds (40.8 kilograms); average 82 pounds (37.2 kilograms)
Arm length—2½ to 3 feet (0.76 to 0.9 meter), about two-thirds of the orangutan's height
Color—Reddish brown. Sumatran males grow white or yellow beards.
Physical Features—Bare face, with round eyes and small ears. Long, shaggy hair that can reach 20 inches (51 centimeters) on shoulder. Long arms; curled fingers and feet; flexible shoulder and hip joints; enormous difference in size between males and females. Males develop large pads on cheeks and large throat pouches.
Distinctive Habits: Lives mainly in trees; swings through branches; males communicate over distance by the long call; males live alone; females live with infant.
Food: Mainly fruit, some leaves, flowers, buds, bark, insects
Reproductive Cycle: Males and females mature at 7 to 10 years; female starts having offspring at 12 years and gives birth every 7 to 9 years; gestation period, 227 to 275 days; female raises young alone; young nurses about 4 years.
Life Span: 35 to 40 years in wild; 50 to 55 in captivity

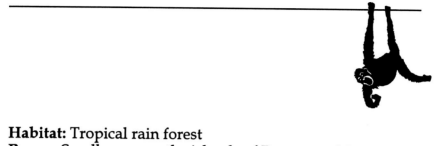

Habitat: Tropical rain forest
Range: Small areas on the islands of Borneo and Sumatra in
    Southeast Asia
Population: 20,000 to 30,000

Sumatran orangutan populations   Bornean orangutan populations

A young orangutan—the "person of the forest"

Chapter 1

The Person of the Forest

Imagine you are deep in a **tropical rain forest***. The trees tower like skyscrapers, nearly shutting out the sun. The air is heavy with heat and moisture. Hundreds of insects—butterflies, cicadas, ants, spiders— fly and buzz and whir around you. You can hear the whoop of monkeys and the twitter of birds.

High above, in the green leaves of a gigantic tree, a tiny infant clings to his large, reddish brown mother. His hairless face peers through the leaves, and his eyes look straight at you.

This animal looks startlingly human.

You have met an orangutan. Its name comes from two words in the Malay language of Southeast Asia: *orang*, "person," and *utan*, "forest." The person of the forest seems so human, especially when young,

*Words in **bold type** are explained in the glossary at the end of this book.

9

that some local legends say the orangutan is descended from wicked men who were turned into beasts for their bad deeds.

Along with the other **great apes**—gorillas, chimpanzees, and bonobos, or pygmy chimpanzees—orangutans are our closest relatives in the animal world. Yet until recently we have known little about them. The African great apes have received far more attention from Western scientists. The islands of Southeast Asia, where the orangutan lives, have been difficult for scientists to reach. And the orangutan is hard to study in its native environment, or **habitat**, because it spends its life hidden in the trees of the dense tropical rain forest.

In the 1960s, interest in the orangutan suddenly grew. For the first time, researchers undertook lengthy **field studies** to watch our fascinating relative in the wild. Today we know far more about the orangutan than we've ever known before. But while our knowledge has increased, the number of orangutans has dramatically decreased. Today scientists

realize that unless drastic measures are taken, the orangutan will soon become **extinct**.

Two Homes for the Orangutan

In **prehistoric** times, orangutans could be found in Asia throughout Borneo and Sumatra, as far north as Beijing, in China, and into India and Java. For unknown reasons, by the time they were first discovered by the Western world in the 1600s, their habitat had been reduced to only two islands: Borneo and Sumatra. Today orangutans live only in small areas on these two islands.

There is one **species**, or kind, of orangutan, and its scientific name is *Pongo pygmaeus*. *Pongo* is an African word that means "ape," and *pygmaeus* is a Latin word that means "short." Scientists **classify** the orangutan species into two smaller groups: the Bornean orangutan and the Sumatran orangutan. The two groups have been living on separate islands for as long as a million years. The last time they might have been in contact was during the last

Ice Age, some 10,000 years ago, when there were land bridges between western Borneo and southern Sumatra.

At first glance, the two groups look the same. The orangutan is a rather awkward-looking, pot-bellied ape, with shaggy red hair, extremely long arms, and short bowlegs. Males, at 4 to 5 feet (1.2 to 1.5 meters) and 165 pounds (74.9 kilograms), are about twice as big as females, who on average grow to be 3½ feet tall (1.06 meters) and 82 pounds (37.2 kilograms). This tremendous contrast in body shape and size between the sexes is called **sexual dimorphism**. Adult males and females look so different that it is always easy to tell them apart. When the male matures, he develops enormous cheek pads on either side of his face, a hanging throat pouch, and a humanlike beard. He looks a bit like a fat old man. The female is so much smaller and lighter that she looks almost like a different kind of ape.

In captivity, where orangutans get less exercise than in the wild, they grow to be much heavier.

Shaggy red hair, very long arms, and short bowlegs characterize *Pongo pygmaeus*.

It's not easy to tell the difference between the Bornean orangutan and the Sumatran orangutan. This mature Bornean male (above) has browner hair and a wider face than the Sumatran male (right).

Some males actually weigh more than 300 pounds (136 kilograms)!

The physical differences between Bornean and Sumatran orangutans are harder to see. Generally, the Bornean has darker hair and a broader face than the Sumatran, and the Sumatran male has a longer, fuller beard. They seem to behave differently, too. In captivity and in the wild, the Sumatran orangutan appears to be more social than the Bornean.

An Animal Like Us

Orangutans are fascinating because they remind us of ourselves. A noted scientist once said about apes, "They are not people—but they are actually not animals either!" Of course, chimpanzees, orangutans, and the other apes *are* animals—but then, so are we. What the scientist meant is that the apes look, act, and think more like humans than do any other animals. In ape faces we can see our own reflections, however different. Naturally, we want to know as much about our relatives as we can.

Chapter 2

The Red Ape

Like monkeys, lemurs, bush babies, other apes, and humans, orangutans are **primates—mammals** with large brains and with fingers and thumbs that can grasp things. Apes are big primates with no tails. (Monkeys are usually smaller, with long tails.) Other apes are the gibbons, siamangs, chimpanzees, bonobos, and gorillas.

About 25 million years ago the first apelike mammals lived somewhere in what is now eastern Africa. Eleven million years later, the ancestors of the orangutans appeared. They were one of a group of primates that **migrated** from Africa across to Europe, Asia, and Southeast Asia. Orangutan teeth and charred bones have been found in Stone Age caves throughout Southeast Asia. Prehistoric humans

With its flexible, powerful limbs, a young orangutan moves easily about the forest canopy.

hunted the red ape and kept the young as pets, just as people do today.

Humans are not descended from apes, but we do share a common ancestor. We are probably most closely related to the modern chimpanzee, with whom we share 98.7 percent of our **genes**. Some humans have even been able to receive blood trans-fusions from chimpanzees. By comparison, we share about 96.7 percent of our genes with the orangutan.

Getting Around

The orangutan lives mostly in the upper branches of the forest **canopy**, 90 to 120 feet (27 to 36 meters) off the ground. It is the largest **arboreal**, or tree-living, animal in existence. It is amazing to think of this big, bulky animal swinging from one fragile branch to another. How can the orangutan move through the treetops without plunging to its death?

Like other primates, the orangutan has flexible hands that can grab and manipulate objects. Its long, curved fingers are built to hook on to small

branches and large trunks—and so are its finger-like toes. In fact, the orangutan essentially has four hands and four arms. Its short legs can move around in circles as easily as its incredibly long arms, which are two-thirds the length of its body. Such flexibility allows it to use any one of its four limbs as an arm.

Orangutans often move by cautiously grasping nearby branches first with one arm, then with the opposite leg, then with the other arm and the other leg, and so on. Sometimes they **brachiate**, or swing hand over hand. Unlike smaller apes or monkeys, orangutans rarely jump or spring from one tree to another. Chances are, the branches wouldn't be able to support their weight, and they would fall.

Although they are not exceptionally fast, orangutans do move easily and even gracefully in trees. But when they travel on the ground, they look slow and awkward. They don't walk on their finger joints, as chimpanzees and gorillas do, but on the sides of

Like humans, the orangutan has long, flexible fingers that can hook on to things and manipulate objects.

their cupped hands and feet, and sometimes on their fists. Shuffling along, they make slow progress. Heavy older males often cover long distances this way. Orangutans hardly ever stand up and walk on just two legs, although they are perfectly capable of doing so, and will often walk across shallow rivers and swamps.

Fruit Eaters

Orangutans are mostly **frugivores**, or fruit eaters. In one year an orangutan may eat hundreds of

different kinds of fruit. They dine on fruits we may have never heard of—strangler figs, and rambutan, and durian, a tough fruit that smells like onions but tastes like almond custard. Some of their foods humans would find inedible, like the strychnos fruit, which contains the poison strychnine. Since each kind of fruit ripens only at certain times during the year, orangutans vary their diet with leaves, bark, flowers, nuts, insects and, rarely, bird eggs. It's possible that they even eat meat when they can get it. A researcher in Borneo once saw a male orangutan eat four baby flying squirrels. Like other apes, and like humans, orangutans are **adaptable** eaters.

Communication

One of the reasons orangutans look so much like humans is that the irises of their eyes are surrounded by white. Most animals have no white in their eyes at all. The orangutan's small, dark eyes can look thoughtful, or curious, or startled, or scared.

Scientists think orangutans can see and hear about as well as we do.

Although they have no spoken language, orangutans do have a body language that helps them communicate moods and desires. Like human faces, orangutan faces are relatively bare of hair, and the eyes, mouth, and brow are very expressive. They have a special face when they are playful, a special face when they are sad, and a special face when they are stressed or angry.

When an orangutan, especially a male, feels threatened, he may react with an angry **display:** grunting, tree-shaking, and branch-breaking.

The sound for which a male orangutan is best known is the **long call**. It is a series of grumbles, roars, and bellows that may last over four minutes and can be heard more than half a mile away. The male may break branches, rattle vines, and shove over dead trees. The long call is basically aggressive: It warns all other males in the area to stay away. But it also lets females know where they can find a mate.

Orangutans have expressive faces. They can look playful, angry, thoughtful, or sad.

Intelligence

The more we learn about the great apes, the smarter we realize they are. They can make and use tools, they can learn from experience, they can reason, and they can even use language. They have the same kind of mental abilities we do, even though these abilities are not as advanced.

Scientists have tested the great apes many times

23

A mature male orangutan on "display"—he makes this fearful face when he is angry or feels threatened.

to measure and compare their intelligence. On some tests orangutans have scored the highest. One even beat a human four-year-old! On other tests, chimpanzees or gorillas have done better. Finally, scientists have decided that the great apes are about equal in intelligence.

The great apes have been observed making and using tools. Wild chimpanzees have been seen stripping long sticks and then poking them into termite nests in order to draw out the tasty insects. Orangutans in the wild have been seen using sticks to scratch their backs. In captivity, they have poked sticks through the hard, spiny skin of the durian to reach the meat of their favorite fruit. One orangutan was even trained to make stone tools to open containers.

The vocal chords of apes cannot make the sounds that we recognize as words. But researchers have worked with chimpanzees and gorillas to teach them American Sign Language (ASL), a series of hand gestures used by the deaf. One gorilla named Koko

In the jungles of Borneo, an adult female named Rinnie makes the correct sign for "leaf" with the encouragement of Gary Shapiro.

has learned more than 600 words. (By comparison, a two-year-old child can usually speak about 250 to 300 words.) One scientist, Gary Shapiro, taught ASL to a number of orangutans in the only study ever done in an ape's natural environment. One young female named Princess learned about 40 signs for words like *food, tickle,* and *hug.*

Scientists think that orangutans could learn as

many words as gorillas or chimpanzees. But since orangutans spend more and more time alone as they get older, they are probably less likely to "talk" as much as their more social cousins.

In another experiment, orangutans passed the "mirror" test. When most animals see their reflection in a mirror, they think they are looking at another animal. Dogs, for instance, will bark at the "strange" dog looking at them. But orangutans, like chimpanzees and dolphins, recognize themselves. This self-awareness is one of the signs of complex thought.

As with any highly intelligent animal, each orangutan has a unique personality, with particular likes, dislikes, and ways of acting. In this book we make general observations about orangutans as a species. But we should always remember that each orangutan is as individual as you or I.

Chapter 3

Living in the Rain Forest

The rain forest where the orangutan makes its home is teeming with life. Hooting gibbons flit through leafy branches; wild pigs wallow in the mud of uprooted trees; 20-foot (6-meter) pythons wait silently beside dark rivers. Animals appear in an amazing variety of shapes and colors: There are long-quilled porcupines, brilliant hornbills, plated pangolins with long sticky tongues, tiny red deer called muntjaks with loud, ferocious barks, and proboscis monkeys with huge red noses.

There have never been many large **predators** (other than people) to threaten the orangutan—and now there are even fewer. Only about 1,000 Sumatran tigers remain in the wild, and the numbers

Gibbons are just one of the amazing multitude of animals that live in the rain forests of Southeast Asia.

of other large cats are also reduced. The stealthy crocodile can be dangerous to the young orangutan. But according to legend, a grown orangutan can kill a crocodile by standing on the reptile's back and ripping open its mouth!

Altogether, it has been estimated that there are 200 species of mammals and 550 species of birds in the Bornean jungle. No one would even attempt to count the millions of kinds of insects.

The climate in the tropical rain forest is hot and wet throughout the year. By the middle of the day, the temperature is usually in the 90s. Still, the forest does have two definite seasons. The rainy season, when great thunderstorms topple trees and swell rivers, lasts from October to April. To escape from the rain, orangutans often hide under shelters that they make by bending leaves and branches.

In the dry season the fruit trees come into bloom. Although the leaves and bark of some trees are available year-round, most of the fruit that the

orangutans eat will ripen between April and October. When its favorite fruits are in season, an orangutan needs to know where to look for them.

Most orangutans live in a **home range** of one-fifth to three square miles (one-half to eight square kilometers). Within its range, each orangutan finds the fruit trees it needs. Females have smaller ranges than males, and these ranges usually overlap with those of other females. They also overlap with those of males. Males generally travel much longer distances than females. Some males don't stay within a home range but go to wherever they can find food and available females.

Orangutans must have a good memory for where fruit will be located throughout the year. The less aimless roaming they do, the more efficiently they use their energy. Mothers show their offspring where fruit is to be found. Naturally, those orangutans with the best memories have the strongest chances of eating well and surviving the longest.

High in the treetops, a female orangutan finds food for herself and her infant.

A Solitary Life

Orangutans live mainly by themselves. The most common orangutan group is a mother and her

infant, occasionally accompanied by an older brother or sister. **Immature** males and females sometimes spend time with their mother or with other young orangutans. But once they grow up, females leave their mother to raise their own babies, and males strike off on their own. Adult males and females come together only to mate.

Naturally, since ranges overlap, neighboring orangutans sometimes meet in their search for food. Adult females, who are probably related, occasionally travel together for short periods of time. When they stop to rest, they may **groom** briefly, picking dirt and insects out of each other's hair. More often, they groom themselves. Nearby, their youngsters may play and chase each other through the trees. After a few hours, or a few days, the two families will go their separate ways. Normally the only time a **mature** male is with other orangutans is when he's accompanied by a female, with or without offspring.

Other apes spend most or all of their time in social groups. Why is the orangutan so solitary?

There are various reasons. The most important requirements for orangutan survival are food and success at raising offspring. Fruit is widely scattered throughout the forest; and since the various fruit trees ripen at different times, it is often scarce. If

orangutans traveled from one tree to another as a group, each orangutan would get less to eat.

Females with young especially need the freedom to move without restriction and eat what they want to. Since they have no serious enemies, they do not need to be protected by the larger males. And they in turn can better protect their offspring if males, who can be aggressive, are not around. Females mate only every seven to nine years, so they don't need male companionship in between.

Clearly, it is to the orangutan's advantage to move independently. Still, every orangutan in an area will at one time or another meet every other orangutan in the area. They recognize and choose their mating partners.

Interestingly, orangutans in zoos are much more involved with one another—looking, playing, grooming—than are those in the wild. Of course, captives are forced to live closer together. Also, they do not have to spend most of their time in search of food. But the difference still shows that, given the

In zoos like this one, captive orangutans live close together and are more sociable than their relatives in the wild.

chance, orangutans can be very social. It's possible that they've become less social over the centuries as their rain-forest habitat has shrunk in size and food has become scarcer.

A Day in the Life

A faint light steals through the gray morning mist. One by one, birds trill a song of welcome. Noisy

gibbons hoot from tree to tree, and swarms of insects start their steady drone. It is the dawn of another day in the rain forest.

In a leafy treetop nest, an orangutan mother and her two-year-old son stir and yawn. Snuggling closer, the youngster nurses briefly. Then they carefully climb together into a neighboring wild plum tree.

She reaches for a fruit and sucks on it, while the youngster runs energetically up and down the branch. Tossing half the fruit away, the mother reaches for another, and still another. Soon the ground beneath the pair is littered with half-eaten fruits and skins.

Orangutans nearly always throw away as much as they eat. Scientists say that this waste actually helps the forest. By discarding fruit, orangutans spread plant seeds. They also help keep trees healthy by eating leaves and buds, and let light into the dense forest by breaking branches.

When they've finished eating, mother and son are ready for the long trip of the day. Swinging or climbing through the trees, they make their way through the upper branches of the forest. The youngster is old enough to travel by himself, though he sometimes climbs on his mother's back or clings to her side. On the way, they crunch on leaves or suck on bark. Once, she dips her hand into the hollow of a tree and scoops out a handful of water, which she drinks thirstily. When they stop to rest, the young one nurses.

Orangutans may travel from 50 to 900 yards (46 to 822 meters) in a single day. Older males, too heavy for the treetops, move on the ground.

When mother and child reach a tree bending under the weight of ripe durians, they find another mother and youngster already eating. The two adults chew noisily but pay little attention to each other. But the young male, happy to have found a friend, starts a game of touch and chase. The two lively orangutans play with each other as the afternoon lengthens.

Shortly after five o'clock, the two families sepa-

Young orangutans love to play with each other—or by themselves.

rate and move into nearby trees. There the mother bends and breaks branches under her feet to make a soft, comfortable nest to sleep in. The youngster tries to make a nest, too, but crawls into hers when she has finished. As dusk falls, they hear the fierce long call of a faraway male. Night comes to the rain forest, and they sleep.

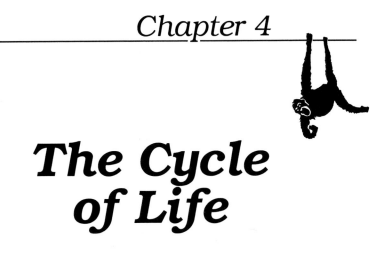

Chapter 4

The Cycle of Life

A weak cry pierces the air. An orangutan mother gazes down at her newborn daughter in wonder. Gently she picks her up and sniffs her, then licks and cleans her tiny body. Soon the infant finds her mother's nipple and begins to nurse.

It is the beginning of a long and loving relationship.

As appealing, and as helpless, as a human baby, a newborn orangutan needs years of loving care and patient teaching in order to survive to adulthood. The pattern of an orangutan's life guarantees that each newborn will receive all the nurturing it needs.

An orangutan infant with its mother. Newborns require years of care before they can be independent.

Courtship and Mating

A female orangutan starts mating at age 7 or 8, but she cannot become pregnant until age 12. Unlike many primates, she can mate during any time of the month and at any time of year. She has some control over her choice of mates. Since orangutans are spread out in a forest, females can often hide from the males they want to avoid. Mature males are especially easy to locate, since they advertise their presence with the noisy long call. Like people, orangutans have strong likes and dislikes. Usually the female prefers full-grown males with impressive cheek pads and beards. The males usually develop these by the age of 15.

Males are known to fight fiercely over females. Adult males have many battle injuries: broken or missing fingers, torn noses, deep scars.

Sometimes females are approached by males, usually young ones, in whom they are not interested. Often they can get away. But sometimes the males mate with them by force. Interestingly,

females rarely become pregnant as a result.

In order for mating to be successful, both male and female must be willing. Orangutans have all sorts of ways to attract each other. They show affection, touching and kissing.

Courting males and females form **consortships** that last anywhere from a few days to several weeks. During this time, the couple travels together, eats the same food, and makes nests in the same trees. It is the longest time adult males and females spend in each other's company. During the consortship, the pair mates often. When the female does become pregnant, the consortship ends. The female avoids males throughout the pregnancy and the baby's infancy.

Being Born

After 8½ months, a tiny (2½- to 3½-pound; 1.1- to 1.6-kilogram) infant is born. She is bald and weak. Although she cannot walk, she has a very strong hand grip, and she clings tightly to her mother.

The mother cuddles her newborn, cleans her fur, and even breathes into her mouth. After about four hours, the infant starts to suckle. She will nurse for four years. Soon she eats fruit that her mother has prechewed. At about one year, she can eat solid food on her own, just like a human baby.

Nearly half the infants born in the wild die before they have a chance to grow up. When this happens, a mother may carry her dead child around for days, holding her tenderly and trying to groom her. When the mother finally puts the body down, she may go into a period of depression that lasts for weeks. She barely eats and shows little interest in her surroundings. We don't know what intelligent animals like apes understand about death. But we do know they can feel unhappiness when one of their own dies.

Growing Up

Young orangs must be taught many things by

Young orangutans need to acquire skills to survive in the rain forest. This youngster is learning to climb.

their mothers—what foods are good to eat, where to find them, what dangers to watch out for. They even have to be taught how to climb. A mother will put an infant on a tree limb to get him used to it. At first the young orangutan may be frightened— all he wants to cling to is his mother's coat! But soon he is scampering along the branches and swinging from the vines.

Orangutans become independent gradually. By the time they're four, they are spending much of their time with other youngsters their own age.

When orangutans grow up, they have to move out of their mothers' ranges because one range cannot provide two adult orangutans with enough food. Daughters establish ranges close by. Males, however, move farther away.

Female orangutans mate and have infants every 7 to 9 years after they first give birth. Since in the wild they don't usually live longer than 40 years, this means that they have only three or four young in their lives. One of the reasons that orangu-

tans are in danger of extinction is that they have so few offspring that manage to survive.

Chapter 5

Saving the Orangutan

Orangutans are in terrible danger. As is the case with so many other species, their numbers have dwindled drastically in this century. Now, as a result of the tremendous surge in human population, they are gradually being squeezed out of living space.

The rain forest where the orangutans live is a place of unparalleled fertility. Today the ancient trees that grow there are being chopped down at an alarming rate. One area on Borneo alone exports almost half of all the tropical wood in the world. Government officials in Borneo sell most of their trees to foreign logging companies in Japan, Taiwan, and Korea. These companies then process the lumber into plywood to make packing crates, cheap furniture, chopsticks, and other household items.

Seriously threatened in their rain-forest habitat, some orangutans are being saved by concerned people.

49

The United States imports some of these products. But the majority are sold in Asia.

Altogether, orangutans have probably lost 80 percent of their habitat to logging and farming. Yet orangutans and other animals are not the only ones who are losing their homes. Native peoples are also being forced off their ancestral lands. Unfortunately, although there is much poverty in Southeast Asia, few of the profits from the sale of wood are used to help ordinary people. Instead, the money remains in the hands of a small group of powerful people. As a result, cutting down the rain forests of Southeast Asia does not lead to the economic development the area needs.

The government does understand the threat to orangutans and other wildlife. It has been steadily increasing the number of protected national parks and reserves, like Tanjung Puting in Borneo and Gunung Leuser in northern Sumatra. Yet even in these protected areas, illegal logging continues to take place.

Loss of habitat is not the only threat to the orangutans. Orangutan infants have traditionally been in much demand as pets in Southeast Asia. Although **poaching** has been illegal for more than 60 years, it is profitable and continues to flourish. In order to capture the infants, hunters must first kill the mothers. Since orangutans are totally dependent on their mothers in the first few years of life, few of the captured orphans survive. They are smuggled out of Indonesia on fishing boats or airplanes, often in tiny wooden boxes.

In 1990, six very ill infant orangutans were found in the Bangkok, Thailand, airport, packed in crates labeled "live birds." Three of them had been packed upside down. Birute Galdikas, a naturalist who has been studying and **rehabilitating** orangutans in Borneo for 23 years, helped return them to the wild. Despite the best care possible, three of them eventually died. Four months later, ten more orphans were discovered while being smuggled into Taiwan. These incidents caused an outcry among

51

A rescued orphan drinks from a cup in a rehabilitation camp in Borneo. For years, orangutan infants have been stolen and sold as pets in Asia.

conservationists all over the world. As a result, poaching has slowed down a bit. Yet orangutan orphans still appear in marketplaces in Taiwan, Singapore, and Thailand each year.

Young orangutans are cuddly and cute. But they do not remain young long—and adult orangutans are dangerous. A mature male is four times—and a mature female three times—as strong as a human male. So when the "pets" grow up, they are either shot, abandoned, or sent to private zoos. The government takes some lucky orphans from their owners

when they're still young and sends them to special rehabilitation camps. There they will be introduced back into the wild.

Since young orangutans rely on their mothers to teach them to survive, orphaned orangutans must be taught by humans how to climb trees, find food, and build nests. At first they are fed bananas and porridge at feeding centers in camp. Gradually, they are led farther away from camp and then left out by themselves overnight. Eventually, it is hoped, they will rejoin the forest around them.

We now know that rehabilitation is not always possible. While some orangutans return completely to the forest, others prefer to spend most of their time in camps. They've become too used to humans ever to be truly wild again.

Visitors love to watch the red-haired apes when they come into camp for their daily feeding. Because orangutans are such a great tourist attraction, the camps are good for the local economy and encourage conservation.

Zoos around the world also have a conservation policy. An international **breeding** program mates Bornean orangutans with other Bornean orangutans, and Sumatrans with other Sumatrans. This way, both groups of orangutans will survive, no matter what happens in the wild. Zoos also play an important role in educating visitors about orangutans. The more people know, the more they will care about their red-haired cousins.

What will the future bring for *Pongo pygmaeus*? It all depends on us. Humans need land. They need food. Because there are so many people, they are crowding out their fellow creatures. Human population growth, already a problem at the end of the twentieth century, may be out of control in the twenty-first. Only through planning and wise use of the land will there be enough room on the planet for everyone.

Orangutans cannot talk, and cannot defend themselves. But they do think, and they do feel, in many ways just like us. Though they run the risk of

Some orangutans get so used to humans that they never completely return to the wild.

extinction, they have a good chance of surviving—if enough people care.

Sources of Information about the Orangutan

Books to Read

Arnold, Caroline. *Orangutan*. New York: Morrow Junior Books, 1990.

Gallardo, Evelyn. *Among the Orangutans: The Birute Galdikas Story*. San Francisco: Chronicle Books, 1993.

Green, Carl R., and William R. Sanford. *The Orangutan*. New York: Crestwood House, 1987.

Montgomery, Sy. *Walking with the Great Apes: Jane Goodall, Dian Fossey, Birute Galdikas*. Boston: Houghton Mifflin Company, 1991.

Organizations to Contact

The Orangutan Foundation International
822 South Wellesley Avenue
Los Angeles, CA 90049-9963
(310) 207-1655

International Primate Protection League
P.O. Box 766
Summerville, SC 29484
(803) 871-2280

Rainforest Action Network
450 Sansome, Suite 700
San Francisco, CA 94111
(415) 398-4404

Glossary

adaptable—able to change or adjust to the environment

arboreal (ar-BOR-ee-ul)—living mainly in trees

brachiate (BRAY-kee-ate)—to move hand over hand from one branch to another

breeding—reproducing young

canopy—the upper level of leafy branches covering a forest

classify—to arrange living things into groups according to their relationships

conservationist (kon-ser-VAY-shun-ist)—one who sees to the careful protection of something, such as animals threatened with extinction, or natural resources like forests, rivers, and minerals

consortship—male and female companionship at mating time

display—a physical show of feelings or aggression meant to threaten another animal

extinct (ehk-STINGKT)—no longer living anywhere on earth

field study—a scientific study of an animal in the wild

frugivore (FROO-ji-vor)—an animal that eats mainly fruit

gene—a tiny part of a cell that passes a characteristic of an animal or plant on to its offspring

great apes—a group of apes consisting of orangutans, gorillas, chimpanzees, and bonobos (pygmy chimpanzees)

groom—to clean oneself; orangutans and other primates sometimes indulge in a friendly social behavior in which one animal cleans another by picking dirt, bugs, and other material out of its fur

habitat—an area where a plant or animal naturally lives

home range—an area that an animal calls its own

immature—not having reached full growth and not yet able to reproduce

long call—the loud, lengthy bellowing call of the male orangutan

mammals—warm-blooded animals that give birth to live young and nurse them with their own milk

mature—having reached full growth and having the ability to reproduce

migrate—to move from one habitat to another in order to breed or feed

poaching—illegally killing or capturing animals

predator (PREHD-uh-tuhr)—an animal that lives by killing and eating other animals

prehistoric—belonging to a time before people started writing history

primates—mammals with large brains and the ability to grasp things with their fingers or toes

rehabilitating (ree-huh-BIL-uh-tate-ing)—introducing animals back into their native habitat

sexual dimorphism (SEK-shu-al dye-MOR-fiz-im)—differences in size and body shape between males and females

species (SPEE-sheez)—a group of animals or plants with many of the same characteristics

tropical rain forest—dense woodlands with a high level of rainfall, located near the equator

Index

Ruth Ashby is a children's book editor, teacher, and writer. Born in Huntington, New York, she studied English literature at Yale University and the University of Virginia and now teaches children's literature and writing part-time at Marymount Manhattan College in New York City. She has written several nonfiction books for young readers, including books on cats, tigers, and sea otters. Ruth Ashby lives in Brooklyn with her husband, their daughter, Rebecca, and their cat, Stoopy.